On Target English

Comprehension and Writing Skills

Year 3

Hilary Frost
Sarah Lindsay
Heather Painter

Longman

Edinburgh Gate
Harlow, Essex

Contents

The Tale of Brave Augustus

Once upon a time an old woman whose name was Mrs Popple lived in a little white cottage among wide green fields. The cottage had a garden where Mrs Popple grew potatoes and onions and cabbages and carrots, and there was a border of flowers on each side of the path that led to the garden gate. Beyond the gate there was a little pond with reeds and rushes by its edge; and on the pond lived Augustus, Mrs Popple's large white gander.

Annette Elizabeth Clark

Mrs Popple and Augustus

1 What colour was Mrs Popple's cottage?

2 What vegetables did Mrs Popple grow in her garden?

3 What grew on each side of the path?

4 Where did Augustus live?

5 What grew at the edge of the pond?

Mrs Popple's cottage

Write the words used in the passage to describe each of these.
The first one is done for you.

1 cottage   *little white*

2 fields

3 woman

4 gander

5 pond

Comprehension

● To find words that describe a setting

Helpful words

reeds potatoes
carrots flowers
pond white
onions cabbages
rushes

Writing

● To write a description of a different setting

Mrs Popple's sister

Mrs Popple had a sister, Mrs Crackle.
Mrs Crackle lived in the town.
This is where she lived.

Remember

A **phrase** is a small group of words about something.

Helpful words

crowded busy flats
tall shops
buses noisy

Tip

The place where a story happens is called the **setting**.

Write some words and phrases about where Mrs Crackle lived.
The first one is done for you.

1 yard   *no pretty flowers*
              not much space
              untidy

2 street

3 buildings

Mrs Crackle's tale

Write four or five sentences to describe the setting for a new story about Mrs Crackle and her little dog.
You can use the words and phrases you have already written.

A Snowy Morning

When the February sun rose behind her house that morning, Jenny was already awake, wrapped in a blanket at the foot of her bed, looking through the icy window.

A new snow covered the backyard. Beyond the fence, the pumpkin field lay white and still. In the distance, skeletons of trees stood, black against the winter sunrise.

Jenny got out of bed and dressed quietly, then tiptoed downstairs so she wouldn't wake her father. She put on her boots and jacket, wrapped a scarf around her neck and mouth, pulled on her mittens, and opened the back door.

The icy air bit her cheeks and brought tears to her eyes as she walked across the yard, making the first footprints of the day in the fresh snow.

From Sky Dancer, *by Jack Bushnell*

Comprehension

- To understand story openings

Snowy morning

Fill the gaps in these sentences:

1 When Jenny looked through the icy _____ she was wrapped in a _____ .

2 _____ covered the back yard and the _____ beyond.

3 The skeletons of _____ looked _____ against the winter sunrise.

4 Jenny tiptoed down the _____ so that she did not wake her _____ .

5 When she walked across the _____ she made the first _____ in the snow.

Helpful words

yard   father
stairs   blanket
trees   footprints
black   field
snow   window

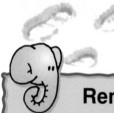

Remember

The **setting** tells where and when the story happens.

Settings

Choose the correct word or words to answer these questions:

1 In which month did the story take place?

December, January, February

2 At what time of day does the story begin?

morning, afternoon, evening

3 What had the weather been like?

foggy, rainy, snowy

4 What was growing in the field?

wheat, pumpkins, potatoes

5 Through which door did Jenny leave the house?

front door, side door, back door

Snowy morning

✏ 1 Look at this picture and write words and phrases that describe the scene.

2 Write some words and phrases describing the boy.

Writing

● To collect ideas to use in a story

Helpful words

Early one morning
bitterly cold
delivering crunching
white blanket
coat boots stalking
excited

Yousef helps out!

✏ Copy the start of the story:

Yousef crept down the stairs, and quietly pulled open the front door. He wanted to be the first to make footprints in the crisp, fresh snow. He looked across the white street, where he saw old Mrs Hall who was halfway down her steps.

Crash! Thump! …

Finish the story by describing what Yousef does to help the old lady.

Try to make something unexpected happen in your story so it is more interesting.

Helpful words

frightened shocked
injured support
assistance emergency
wrapped warm
freezing

Tip
Your story needs a title.

9

Unusual Poems

Thoughts in a launderette

My washing's going round and round I left that red sock in it's dyeing Matthew's shirt and Ian's football kit he'll kill me what will mum say will mum say about the pink pillowcases I'll say the lady put them in for me yes that's what I'll say . . .

Rita Ray

Friendly warning

LISTEN GRASS, TAKE IT EASY. DON'T GROW TOO TALL. THEY'LL JUST BRING IN A LAWN MOWER AND CUT YOU DOWN SHORT.

SEE? I TOLD YOU THEY WOULD.

Robert Froman

Thoughts in a launderette

Read the poem *Thoughts in a launderette* by Rita Ray.
Write the beginnings of these sentences in your book and finish them:

1 Matthew will be upset because ...

2 Ian will be cross because ...

3 Mum will be cross because ...

4 I will blame it on ...

Comprehension

● To understand shape poems

Helpful words

lady red
dyed football kit
pink pillowcase
sock shirt

Friendly warning

Read the poem *Friendly warning* by Robert Froman.
Copy into your book the sentences that are true:

The poet is talking to the grass.

The poet shows the grass is getting taller by making the letters bigger.

The poet is talking to the mower.

The poet is warning the grass not to grow.

The letters get smaller when the grass is cut.

Tip

The shape of a **shape poem** reminds you what it is about.

Writing

- To write a shape poem

Word shapes

Some words can be written in a way to remind the reader of their meaning.

Write these words in a way to remind the reader of their meaning.

> small   lift   jump   long   snake   explosion

Choose three more to add to your list.

Tip

Practise the words first on a scrap of paper before writing them in your book.

Balloons

Write a shape poem about balloons.

First you will need to collect words and phrases about balloons.

Start like this.

> round   float   in the sky   lighter than air

Choose the ones you like best to use for your balloon poem.

Write it in a balloon shape like this.

Remember

A **phrase** is a group of words about something.

Balloons

by

Little Red Riding Hood Goes to Town

We all know the story of Little Red Riding Hood, but what happened to her when she moved to the town?

Little Red Riding Hood's mother was worried about all the dangers in the forest. Little Red Riding Hood loved living in the country but thought it would be good to move to a place where she could play with other children. Her new home was on the fourth floor of a block of flats. From her balcony she could see far across the town, over the houses, the offices, the shops, far away to the forest beyond.

Comprehension

- To answer questions about a picture and a text

Remember

Use a **capital letter** for the first letter in each name.

Helpful words

forest floor
houses children
fourth flats
school church
dangers offices
shops play

From Little Red Riding Hood's window

Look at the picture on page 13.
Write the information in your book.

1 Make a list of six different buildings you can see in the picture.

2 How many cars can you see?

3 What is Little Red Riding Hood's pet?

4 Choose a name for her pet.

5 What is the name of the school?

Little Red Riding Hood thinks about her new home

Write a sentence to answer each question:

1 Why did Little Red Riding Hood's mother want to move to the town?

2 Why did Little Red Riding Hood want to live in the town?

3 Where was her new home?

4 What do you think she felt when she looked at the far away forest?

Little Red Riding Hood in the town

Write these sentences in your book.
Fill the gaps with your own ideas.

Little Red Riding Hood lives in the town. From the balcony of her flat she can hear the sound of _____. One day she decides to go to _____. She feels very _____. Suddenly she sees _____. Now she feels _____.

More about Little Red Riding Hood

What happens next in this story?
Does something dangerous happen?
Does she return safely to her flat?

Write some more sentences to finish the story.
Make your story exciting.

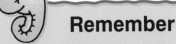 **Writing**

- To write another adventure about Little Red Riding Hood

Helpful words

cars   lorries
traffic   shops
school   park
happy   sad
excited   worried
frightened

Remember

A sentence starts with a **capital letter** and ends with a **full stop**.

15

The Olympics

lit at the beginning of every games

jumping

flags of all the countries taking part

warming up

The first Olympic Games took place nearly 3000 years ago in Greece. Now the Olympics are held every four years. Each time they are in a different country.

At the Olympic Games sportsmen and sportswomen from all over the world compete against each other to see who is the very best in the world at each sport.

In the beginning there were only a few events, like running and boxing. Now the Olympic Games have many more events with thousands of people taking part.

The modern Olympic Games

Write the beginnings of these sentences in your book.
Choose the right endings from the box below.

1 Every four years

2 The first Olympic Games

3 Running and boxing

4 Today thousands of people

took place in Greece.
take part in the Olympic Games.
the Olympic Games are held.
were early events.

In the stadium

1 What three events are taking place in the stadium?

2 Do men and women compete in the Olympic Games?

3 Why are there flags around the stadium?

4 Why do you think the competitors need to warm up before taking part?

Helpful words

muscles   sprinting
countries   damage
jumping   throwing

throwing

sprinting

17

Writing

● To make a record of events

Using information

You have been asked to write some information about the Olympic Games for the children in another class.

Use the information in the text and the picture on pages 16 and 17 to finish these sentences. Make them as interesting as possible.

Set out your work like this, using headings:

The Olympic Games

   The Olympic Games first started _____.

   The Olympic flame _____.

   The flags _____.

Next, make a list of the events.

The events

   Running

If you know any more Olympic sports, add them to your list.

Tip

Headings make it easier for readers to find the information they need

Tip

You could use an **encyclopedia** or **information books** to find more facts.

The Union Jack

The British flag is called the Union Jack. What does the British flag look like?

Find it in the picture.

Draw it in your book and name it.

Time to Get Up!

Comprehension

● To understand the sequence of a story

Get up Tom!

These sentences are in the wrong order.
Write them in your book in the right order.

Mum is shouting at Tom from the bottom of the stairs.

Tom says, "I wish I was still in bed."

Tom is fast asleep in bed.

The teacher says, "Come on Tom, we were waiting for you!"

Tom's breakfast is ready in the kitchen.

Tom hates mornings!

Fill the gaps and finish the sentences in your own words:

<table>
<tr><td>

Helpful words

cross   work
stay   late
tidy   untidy
clothes   floor

</td><td>

1 Tom's mum is feeling _____ because _____.

2 Tom wishes _____ because _____.

3 Tom finds it difficult to find his clothes because _____.

</td></tr>
</table>

 **Writing**

● To identify speech

Story and speech

In the story some of the writing is **about the story** while other parts are telling us **what is said**.

 Sort the writing from these pictures and the others on page 19 into the correct column, like this.

Telling us about the story	Telling us what is said
Tom is fast asleep in bed.	Where is Tom? He's going to be late!

Tom likes playtime!

Draw a picture of Tom with his friends at playtime. Give each person a speech bubble.

Underneath, write a sentence about the picture.

Write in the speech bubbles what the people in your picture are saying.

 Remember

You should not use speech marks in a speech bubble.

The Telly is Watching You

Ben and Shani were best friends and often, after school, they would go home together and watch TV.

"Try another channel," Shani said, through a mouthful of cake. "This is awful."

When she said this, the TV screen glowed a little less brightly as if disappointed.

Ben blopped the blopper. Now the screen showed horse racing.

"Boring!" said Shani.

"No, wait a mo, let me see who wins," said Ben.

"Rotten old horses," said Shani. "Who needs them?"

They forgot the telly to have a quarrel.

Ben said, "You always want things your own way!"

And Shani sang, "Boring, boring, boring!"

The screen went dimmer and dimmer, almost as if it were sad to be ignored.

Nicholas Fisk

Watching TV

1 What did Ben and Shani do after school?

2 What was Shani eating?

3 What was Ben doing when he 'blopped the blopper'?

4 Which programme did Ben like but Shani did not?

5 What did Ben and Shani quarrel about?

 Comprehension

● To understand the feelings of characters

> **Helpful words**
>
> programme
> horse racing
> television
> cake channel

Feelings

1 How do you think Shani and Ben were feeling when they got home?

2 How did the TV feel when Shani and Ben didn't like the programmes?

3 How did Shani feel when Ben wanted to watch horse racing?

> **Helpful words**
>
> happy angry
> strange bored
> sad cross
> disappointed

23

Writing

● To write a simple play script

Tip

The people in the play are called the **characters**.

Writing a play

When a story is changed into a play we set things out in a different way.

First we write the character's name and then we write what they say.

Who speaks (characters)	What they say
Shani	Try another channel, this is awful.
Ben	No, wait a mo, let me see who wins.

Write in your book the next part of the play.
Set it out like this:

Shani _____

Ben _____

Shani _____

Remember

We don't use **speech marks** when we write a play.

What happens next?

Write some more lines of your own. Remember to write who is speaking the words.

Party Time!

Cornflake Slices

Ingredients

- $1\frac{3}{4}$ cups of cornflakes
- 1 cup of coconut
- $1\frac{1}{2}$ cups of rolled oats
- $\frac{3}{4}$ cup of castor sugar
- 125 g of soft butter
- 2 tablespoons of honey

Instructions

1 Grease a baking tray with some butter.

2 Mix in a bowl the cornflakes, coconut, rolled oats and sugar.

3 Add the soft butter and honey. Mix all the ingredients together.

4 Spread the mixture on to the baking tray.

5 Turn the oven on to 180°C / 375°F.

6 When the oven is hot, put in the baking tray for 20 minutes.

7 Let the baking tray cool.

8 Cut into slices.

TAKE CARE!
Only ever use a hot oven when an adult is with you.

25

Comprehension

- To understand how to use recipes

Time to help

1 Carl is collecting together the things to make Cornflake Slices for his party but he has forgotten three ingredients.
Make a list in your book of what he has forgotten.

2 Something has been spilt on Carl's recipe. Help him out by answering these questions:

a What does he need to mix in his bowl?

b What does he do after he has mixed all the ingredients together?

c How long does he need to cook the Cornflake Slices in the oven?

Hunt the sweets

Helpful words

fruit   third
among   shelf
bowl   plant
growing

Carl has hidden lollies around the party room.
He has written the clue for the first one:

Under the table but not on the floor.

Write the clues for the other three lollies.

Pass the parcel

Carl has to get the parcel ready for *Pass the parcel*.
Write some instructions to help him.
Here are some headings to help you.

What things you need

- _____
- _____
- _____

What you need to do

1 _____
2 _____
3 _____

 ### Writing

- To write instructions for games

Helpful words

*sticky tape   wrap
layers   newspaper
forfeit   prize*

 Remember

Don't forget to number your instructions in the right order.

Party games list

Carl needs to get four games ready for his party.

Help him to make a list of what is needed to play each game.

Draw this table in your book and fill it in.

Hunt the sweet. Musical bumps. Musical statues. Pin a tail on the donkey. Pass the parcel.

Game	What is needed
Pin a tail on the donkey	• picture of a donkey • a tail with a pin • a blindfold

Robin Hood Meets Little John

These picture storyboards have been muddled.

Beside the stream.

I'm Little John. Pleased to meet you, but next time remember, 'more haste, less speed'.

A big man like this would be good to have as a friend.

Soaking wet, dripping.

Little John helps Robin out of the water.

A woodland path reaches a stream. The only way across is over a small bridge.

Stand back, young man!

No! I'm in a hurry, and anyway I was crossing the bridge first.

Narrow, log bridge.

Robin and Little John meet on the bridge.

Back at the camp the tables are set up for the feast and everything is ready.

I am pleased to be joining you all.

These are my merry men.

Delicious, fresh food.

Robin brings Little John to his camp where he is welcomed by all the men.

Deep in the forest at Robin Hood's camp.

I think I'll go for a walk before the feast is ready.

Leafy, green forest. Bright sunny day.

Friar Tuck is busy getting ready for the feast.

On the bridge.

Ugh! Help!

Ouch!

Sword, wooden staff.

Both men fight to see who will cross the bridge first.

Action!

The storyboards on the facing page are in a muddle.
Below each picture is written the **action** that is taking place.

Write the action sentences in the correct order.

Start like this:

1 Friar Tuck is busy getting ready for the feast.

You have now written an **outline** of the story.

Settings

The **setting** is written above the pictures.
Write in your book the settings in the right order.

Start like this:

1 Deep in the forest at Robin Hood's camp

Comprehension

● To sequence storyboards

Tip

The **action** is what people are doing.

Remember

The **setting** tells where and when the story happens.

29

Writing

● To write another adventure for Robin Hood

Robin Hood to the rescue!

These pictures tell a story.

The **setting** and the **characters** are the same as in the first story.

Write some **action** sentences to say what is happening in each picture.

Start your story like this:

> One day Robin and Little John were going for a walk in the forest when they saw _____.

Helpful words

Robin Hood   poor man
Little John
soldiers   stealing
sacks of flour
fighting   chasing
eating   sharing

Sayings

1 In your own words, write what this saying means.

> More haste, less speed.

2 Write a sentence to say what each of these sayings means:

Better late than never.
A stitch in time saves nine.
A friend in need is a friend indeed.

The Dragon and the Cockerel

This is the beginning of a Chinese legend.

Every New Year all the animals spent weeks getting ready and making their costumes for the parties. Everyone was happy – well, nearly everyone …

Only Dragon was miserable. He felt himself to be the most dull and boring creature in all China. You see, in those days Dragon had the head of a camel, the eyes of a demon, the neck and body of a snake, the legs of a tiger and the claws of an eagle. But the fact that he had nothing on top of his head caused him the greatest shame.

One day, as Dragon was swimming in the river, Cockerel came strutting by. Cockerel looked magnificent with his gorgeous tail fanned open and those huge antlers on top of his head. Dragon looked longingly at the antlers.

Comprehension

- To sort out descriptions

Magnificent or miserable?

The beginning of this story tells us what the Dragon and the Cockerel look like.

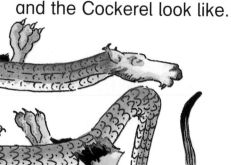

Copy this table into your book.
Sort these phrases into the correct column.
The first one is done for you.

eyes of a demon   gorgeous tail
claws of an eagle   legs of a tiger
body of a snake   huge antlers

Dragon	Cockerel
eyes of a demon	

Remember

A sentence begins with a **capital letter** and ends with a **full stop**.

Helpful words

miserable swimming
China nothing
head river
shame wanted

About the story

1 Where does this story come from?

This story comes from _____.

2 How did the Dragon feel?

3 What caused him 'the greatest shame'?

4 Where was the Dragon when he saw the Cockerel?

5 Why did the Dragon look 'longingly' at the antlers?

The Mojo Bird

Invent another character for this story. It is called the Mojo Bird.

1 First you need to think what a Mojo Bird might look like. You can describe different parts of it like this.

a **thin**, **sharp**, **pointed** beak

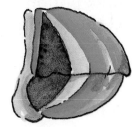

or a **thick**, **colourful**, **powerful** beak

Write descriptive phrases about its

● beak   ● claws
● feathers   ● eyes.

2 Draw a picture of your bird and label the different parts.

More about the Mojo Bird

Write some sentences in your book about the Mojo Bird, describing what it is like.
Then write about where it lives and what it eats.

Helpful words

*kind and friendly
nosy,
wants to know everything
shy and frightened
noisy and clumsy
nasty and sly
dreamy and forgetful*

Firefighters to the Rescue

Always ready

Each year over one million telephone calls are made to fire stations in this country.

The firefighters rescue people from burning buildings and put out fires. They need to be very fit and brave.

Fire!

When the alarm bell rings, the firefighters run to their fire engines. In the fire engines they put on special clothing and helmets to protect them from the fire.

The most important job

When the firefighters reach the fire the most important thing is to make sure nobody is trapped in the burning building. Sometimes they need to wear special masks and breathing apparatus so they can enter rooms that are full of thick, choking smoke.

Long ladders may be used to reach anyone trapped high up in a building.

Stopping the fire

Next the firefighters pump large amounts of water, or foam, into the fire. Sometimes they also need to spray nearby areas to stop the fire from spreading.

When the fire is out the firefighters help clear up. Then they drive back to the station, often very tired, and wait for the next emergency call.

About firefighters

1 How many telephone calls are made to fire stations each year?

2 What do the firefighters do when the alarm bell rings?

3 What do they do when they are in the fire engine?

4 How do the firefighters enter rooms filled with smoke?

5 How do they reach people trapped high up in buildings?

6 What do they do after the fire has been put out and before they go back to the fire station?

 Comprehension

● To make notes from a text

Helpful words

ladders breathing
clothes million
special clear up
engines masks
helmets apparatus

Making notes

Write in your book four facts about firefighters. Use the information and the pictures to help you.

Use this heading and write a fact beside each bullet point. The first is done for you.

Firefighters

● Firefighters wear protective clothing.

●

●

●

Writing

● To write lists and instructions

In school

You need a notice for your classroom to remind everyone what to do when the fire alarm goes.

Write the instructions in your book. Make them simple and clear.

First, write this heading:

What to do when the alarm sounds

Then write the instructions like this:

1 *When the alarm sounds, stand up and walk quietly to the door.*

Remember

Number your instructions.

Dangers at home

Look carefully at this picture. It shows many dangerous things that could start a fire or cause an accident.

Write a sentence to describe why some things are dangerous, and a sentence for each saying how it can be made safe, like this:

The clothes drying near the fire are dangerous because they might catch alight.

Clothes can be dried safely if they are hung up well away from the fire.

Helpful words

cooker   repaired
catch   trip
wires   electricity
lamp   move
light

Saint George and the Dragon

First paragraph

Long ago there was a fearsome
dragon. He lived in the countryside
outside a town. If the people didn't
feed him the dragon would burn their
crops. So, to keep him happy, each
day they sent a sheep for the dragon
to eat, until one day there weren't
any sheep left.

Second paragraph

The worried king called a meeting in
the town square to decide what
should be done. An old woman
suggested that instead of sheep,
people should be sent. Lots were
drawn to decide who would be the
first to be fed to the dragon.

Third paragraph

The princess was the first one chosen.
As she walked out through the gate
the king was distraught, but there
was nothing he could do! All the
townsfolk were watching from the
wall as the dragon approached the
young girl. She pleaded for her life,
but he took no notice and was just
about to devour her when …

Glossary

fearsome   *frightening*

Lots were drawn   *picking
    one name out from all
    the names*

distraught   *very upset*

pleaded   *begged*

devour   *eat greedily*

Comprehension

- To find information in paragraphs

Remember

Sentences begin with a **capital** letter and end with a **full stop**.

Helpful words

distraught instead
worried sheep
town square people
lots decide
dragon

Paragraphs

The beginning of this story is divided into three parts. Each part is called a **paragraph**.

1 In which paragraph does it tell us that the dragon would burn the crops if the people didn't feed him?

2 In which paragraph do the people of the town draw lots?

3 In which paragraph is the king very upset?

4 Which paragraph is the picture about?

The meeting

1 Where did the king call a meeting?

2 What did the old woman suggest?

3 Did the people of the town agree with the old woman?

4 What word is used to describe the king when he calls the meeting?

5 What word is used to describe how upset the king felt when the princess had to go to the dragon?

Making storyboards

This is a storyboard of the first paragraph.

Setting

Speech

In the countryside outside a town

I want more food!

Each day they sent a sheep for the dragon to eat

Action

Tip

Your answers for *The meeting* on page 38 will help you.

✏ Make your own storyboard, like this, for the second paragraph.

Draw a picture first and then do the writing.

Saint George to the rescue

✏ Make a storyboard for the end of the story. Don't forget to say what Saint George did.

The Good Friend

Long ago, before cars, trains or buses, a man went on a journey. On the way down a hot and dusty road, he was attacked. He was badly hurt and his money was stolen.

Soon, a group of holy men came by. They were busy and in a hurry, so they pretended not to see the injured man.

A little later, along the same road came a stranger. He saw the injured man and went quickly to help him. He cleaned his wounds and took him to a nearby inn where he arranged for the man to rest until he felt better. When he was sure the man was well again the stranger carried on with his journey.

A dangerous journey

Match the beginnings and endings of these sentences.

1 A man set out on a journey

once he was sure the man was well.

2 A group of holy men came by

then took him to a nearby inn.

3 The stranger cleaned his wounds

and on the way he was attacked.

4 The stranger carried on with his journey

but pretended not to see the man.

Thinking about the story

1 Why didn't the holy men help the man?

2 What do you think about the stranger's action?

3 What lesson is the story giving us?

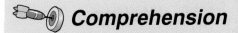

Comprehension

● To write your own opinions clearly

Helpful words

busy kind helpful
hurry help
friend care

41

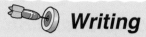

Writing

● To plan a story

Plans

This is a plan of the story you have just read.

Title	The Good Friend
Setting	a hot, dusty and deserted road
Characters	the traveller a group of holy men the stranger
What happens	The man is attacked and hurt.
Resolution	The stranger looks after him.

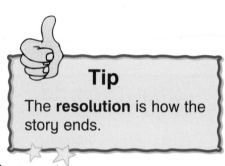

Tip

The **resolution** is how the story ends.

Here is the beginning of another story:

> One day last week there was a robbery at the bank near your school.
>
> The robbers ran through the playground while trying to escape, then something unexpected happened.

Make a plan for the whole story. The setting is done for you.

Tip

Don't have too many characters in your story.

Title	
Setting	the playground, one day last week
Characters	
What happens	
Resolution	

Using the plan

Use your plan to write the story in your book.

Making a Musical Instrument

How to make a shaker

What you need

- 2 yoghurt pots

- rice or pasta

- sticky tape

- paints and a paint brush

What you do

1 Put some rice or pasta into one of the yoghurt pots.

2 Fix the second yoghurt pot to the pot containing the rice or pasta, using the sticky tape.

3 Paint your shaker in bright colours. Let it dry.

43

Comprehension

- To select accurate statements

Writing instructions

Match the beginnings and endings of these sentences.

The main heading	to show in which order to do things.
The bullet points	tells us what is to be made.
The instructions are numbered	help to make the instructions clear.
Diagrams	are short, quick phrases.

Playing together

Helpful words

drums   dreadful
triangles   noise
conductor   shakers
chime bars   cymbals

Look at this picture and then answer the questions.

1 Name three musical instruments that you can see in the picture.

2 Is the music noisy or quiet?

3 What do you think a teacher might be thinking?

4 What do we call the child who is standing at the front?

Making a musical scraper

To make a scraper I need to get an empty plastic bottle, some elastic bands and a lolly stick.

First, I paint the bottle with bright colours and then I must put the elastic bands firmly around the empty bottle. To make the scraping sound, I scrape with the lolly stick down the bottle.

I will jot down how to make a scraper.

Writing
● To make notes

To make notes we need to write down key words and phrases.

Use the key words and phrases to help you write instructions for making a musical scraper.

What you need	What you do
●	1
●	2
●	3

Tip

The words in red are the **key words** and **phrases**.

Making a drum

How could you make a drum?
Jot down your ideas on a piece of paper.

Now write the instructions in your book.
First write a list of what you need.
Then write the instructions in the right order.

Remember

The instructions should be numbered.

45

Gulliver's Travels

Spot the mistake

Correct the mistakes in these sentences.

1 Gulliver rowed his boat to the island.

2 The little people used spears to attack Gulliver.

3 The king was wearing a red cloak.

4 The little people would not give Gulliver any food.

5 Gulliver escaped towards the mountains.

How they felt

1 Pretend you were Gulliver. Write one word to say how you felt when:

- the ship you were on struck the rocks.

- you saw an island nearby.

- you reached the warm sand of the beach.

- you woke and found yourself tied up.

- you were looking at the king.

2 Pretend you were one of the little people.
Fill the gaps in these sentences with one or more words.

When we saw the huge giant swimming towards our island we felt _____ and so we _____.

When we realised he was not wanting to harm us we felt _____ and so we _____.

When he tried to escape we felt _____ and so we _____.

Comprehension

- To undertand the feelings of characters

Helpful words

swam beef
sea blue
bows and arrows

Helpful words

terrified scared
pleased relieved
delighted surprised
puzzled confused
worried frightened

Helpful words

chased threatened
afraid frightened
relieved angry
disappointed cross

Writing

- To plot a sequence of episodes

Remember

An **episode** is a section, or part of, a story.

Planning the Gulliver story

To plot a sequence of **episodes** in a story, you need to know all the things that are going to happen.

The pictures on page 46 tell the story of Gulliver. They show the most important things that happen in each part of the story.

Write a sentence to say what is happening in each picture.

Number your sentences to match the pictures.

The boy who cried wolf

These sentences describe the different episodes in this story, but they have been muddled up.

Write them in the right order so that you have made a plan of the story.

Tip

The story starts because the boy is bored. He tries to add some excitement to his life but it backfires!

- When the villagers heard the boy's call, they rushed to help him but they found there was no wolf.

- The villagers would not go to help because they thought the boy was lying again.

- He pretended a wolf was attacking his sheep, and called for help.

- A wolf attacked the sheep and the boy called for help.

- As the boy watched his sheep he became bored.

The Tale of Thomas Mead

There was a boy called Thomas Mead
who never ever learned to read.
"I wish you would!" his teacher sighed.
"Why should I?" Thomas Mead replied.

Well, one day Thomas went out walking.
He heard the men above him talking,
but couldn't read the sign that said,
"DANGER – workmen overhead."

A pot of paint fell through the air,
and changed the colour of his hair.
"Can't you read?" the workmen cried.
"Why should I?" Thomas Mead replied.

Pat Hutchins

DANGER
workmen
overhead

Comprehension

- To understand the meanings of words

Get it right

Choose the correct answer to each of these questions:

1 Who could not read?

The workmen could not read.
Thomas Mead could not read.

2 What did his teacher say?

I wish you would.
Why should I?

3 What could Thomas Mead hear when he went out walking?

He could hear the workmen working.
He could hear the workmen talking.

4 What was written on the sign?

BEWARE — falling pots of paint.
DANGER — workmen overhead.

Find the word

Copy these lists and draw a line to join the words with a similar meaning:

Remember

A **synonym** is a word with a similar meaning.

Author's word	Similar word
replied	can
overhead	chatting
walking	notice
sign	strolling
talking	answered
pot	above

Why is reading important?

Thomas Mead did not want to learn to read.
List four reasons why you think it would help him to be able to read. The first one is done for you.

Some reasons why Thomas Mead should learn to read

● *He could read warning signs and avoid getting hurt.*

Helpful words

enjoy   stories
information   notices
danger   instructions
signs   accidents
letters   books

Writing a letter

Write a letter to Thomas Mead for his mother to read to him.

Try to persuade him that it is important and enjoyable to be able to read.

10 Hillside Rd
Barton
Bartonshire
BT5 7SC

25th August

Dear Thomas,

   I really think you should learn to read.
There are several reasons.

First, ...

Remember

Set out your letter carefully in the correct way.

51

Children in Roman Times

At school

In Roman times only boys from rich families went to school. They first went to school when they were six or seven years of age.

School started very early in the morning.

At school the boys were taught to read and write, and to do sums.

After lessons had finished they did sports, including running, wrestling and fencing. The Romans thought it was important to be fit at all times.

The teachers were very strict and schoolboys had to behave well.

Games and toys

Roman children played games with hoops, rolling and throwing them. They also pretended they were grown up and would play at chariot racing, with the older children sometimes using little carts pulled by donkeys.

When they were inside their homes, children would make models and play with dolls.

Roman baths

It was fun going to the baths. Children met their friends, and swam and played in the warm water, but they also had to wash and bathe before going home.

Roman children

1 At what age did Roman children start school?

2 Which children went to school?

3 What did Roman children learn at school?

4 What did the children do after lessons?

5 What toys did the Roman children have?

6 What did the children do before going home from the Roman baths?

Being a Roman child

Answer these questions and don't forget to explain your reasons:

1 What would you like most about being a child in Roman times?

2 What would you least like about being a child in Roman times?

 Comprehension

● To scan a text for information

Helpful words

read six rich hoops
carts fencing wrestling
write seven running
bathes sums
dolls wash

Tip

The word **because** could be useful.

Writing

- To make and use notes

Remember

Notes do not have to be full sentences. They are words that remind you of the facts.

Making notes

1 Your friend is away from school because of a broken arm, and has asked you to tell her what you have done and learnt in school today.

Write some notes under each heading to remind you what you have learnt about the Romans today.

Set out your notes like this:

At school

only rich boys ...

—————————

Games and toys

hoops

—————————

Roman baths

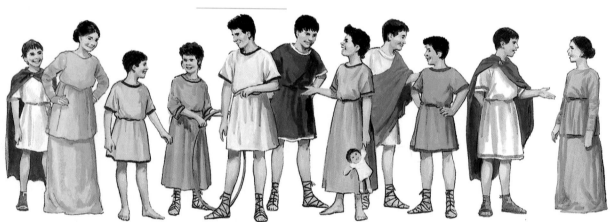

2 Look at these pictures and make some notes about what Roman children wore.

Use the title *Clothes*.

Using your notes

Use your notes to help you write some interesting sentences about how Roman children dressed.

Your writing, and a picture, could go in a book about Roman children.

54

Superpooch

This is a little house, in a little street, in the little town of Wittering. There is nothing special about it. Maybe, maybe not.

This is Mrs May's dog who lives there. He has long ears, a stumpy tail and sleepy eyes. Nothing special about him. Maybe, maybe not.

They say his name is Poochie.

Sometimes it is. Sometimes it isn't.

This is Chatwin, the cat. Chatwin is a cat who knows the town. She knows everything that goes on. No maybes. She *knows*.

She is the one who knows the secret of Poochie's two names. Sleepy Poochie is really **SUPERPOOCH!**

Pat Thompson

Comprehension

- To recognise the words used to create an effect

Mrs May's pets

Mrs May has two pets.
Copy this table in your book.
Fill in the information from the story.

Pet	Name	Where it lives	What it is like
dog			
cat			

What do you think?

1 In the story you can find two answers to each of these questions.

Write the words the author uses to answer these questions.

The first one is done for you.

- Is there something special about the house in the town of Wittering?

  Maybe, maybe not.

- Is there something special about Mrs May's dog?

- Is his name Poochie?

2 When Poochie becomes Superpooch he changes.

Copy this table and write at least four adjectives in each of the columns.

Two are done for you.

Poochie	Superpooch
timid	adventurous

Remember

Adjectives are **describing** words.

Helpful words

noisy   quiet   sleepy
brave   ordinary   busy

Poochie and Superpooch

Writing

- To select words carefully to create an effect

Helpful words

home   quietly   asleep
basket   sunny   peaceful
Chatwin   cleaning

Helpful words

suddenly   changing
strong   brave   quickly
dashing   racing   rescue

Look at this picture.

Write a story about Superpooch.

- Start by setting the scene when he is still Poochie.

- Start a new paragraph when Poochie changes into Superpooch. Make this part of your story exciting.

- At the end of your story don't forget to change Superpooch back into Poochie.

Superpooch to the rescue

This could be the title of your story, or you might think of a better one.

Read and edit your story.

When you are really pleased with it, copy it out in your best handwriting.

Remember

When you edit your work you need to:

- change words and phrases to make clearer sentences
- check your punctuation
- check your spellings are correct.

Fun Poems

Dick's Dog

Dick had a dog
The dog dug
The dog dug deep
How deep did Dick's dog dig?

Trevor Millum

Elephant

Have you ever seen an elephant
Sitting down to dinner?
If you saw how much he eats
You'd know why he's not thinner.

Sonia Higgs

Penguin

Big flapper
Belly tapper
Big splasher
Fish catcher
Beak snapper.

Rebecca Clark (aged 8)

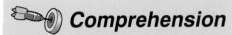

Thinking about the poems

1 Find a word in the poems that rhymes with:

   a dinner

   b snapper

2 Next to each word in question 1, write two other words that rhyme.

   The first should be a real word, and the second an invented word of your own.

Tip

Words that have **rhyming sounds** can have different letter patterns.

3 Draw and finish this table in your book.

Title of poem	Dick's Dog		Penguin
Number of lines			
Lines that rhyme	None	2nd and 4th	
Poet's name		Sonia Higgs	

The one I like best

Which poem do you like the most?
Write three reasons why you like it.

Helpful words

funny
word sounds help your imagination
lots of words that rhyme
asks a question and gives an answer
is difficult but fun to say

Writing

- To write sound poems and tongue twisters

Remember

Give your poem a title.

Tip

Use the pictures to help you think of ideas.

Watery sounds

squelching feet
leaky taps
soaking clothes
sloshing buckets

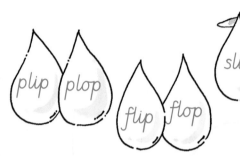

plip plop
flip flop
slip slop
drip drop

Use the words to make a sound poem.
Start like this:

Leaky taps, plip, plop.

_____

_____

_____

Tongue twisters

Tongue twisters usually have lots of words that start with the same sound (*dog, dug, dig, deep*).

Here are some words and phrases about snails:

sailing snails   snoring snails   slipping snails
spinning snails   skipping snails   skidding snails

Write a tongue twister poem about snails.
Can your friend read it quickly without making a mistake?

Road Accident

I can't believe it!
I was just turning on the radio.
When I looked up I was driving straight
for the café.
I couldn't stop! I just couldn't stop!
I'm so sorry.

We were sitting there eating our cakes.
Suddenly there was a huge crash, and the
whole building shook.
I hid my head under my hands.
I thought I was going to be killed!
Then everything went very still and quiet.
When the dust cleared, there was a lorry
parked right next to the table!

We were playing football when we heard
a big bang!
All we could see were people rushing
everywhere and clouds of dust and steam.
We rushed across to the café
to see if we could help.

Comprehension

- To summarise what is happening

What really happened

Write these sentences in your book.
Write *true*, *false* or *can't tell* next to each one.

1 The lorry driver was turning on his radio.

2 The children were on their way to school.

3 The lorry driver was trapped in the cab.

4 The people in the cafe were eating cakes.

5 The lorry driver was travelling to London.

Police questioning

A police officer has arrived at the scene.
Answer these questions as if you were the people.

Helpful words

turning radio rushing
table bang
crash parked driving
suddenly   steam

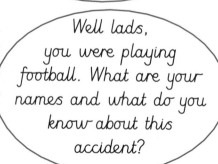

Well, Mr Brown, how did you come to drive your lorry into that cafe?

I was just _____
_____
_____ .

Well, Mr and Mrs Snow, you were sitting in the cafe. What did you see and hear when the accident happened?

We were having tea when _____
_____
_____ .

Well lads, you were playing football. What are your names and what do you know about this accident?

I'm Jim and he is Rudy. We were in the middle of a game of football when
_____
_____
_____ .

Writing the report

The police officer has collected some information about the accident and she needs to write a report.

Copy and fill in this report sheet.

Name of person interviewed
Mr Brown

What they were doing

What they saw

What they heard

Do a report sheet for each of the other witnesses.

Remember

Only include the facts that are known.

Writing a letter

Imagine you are one of the children. Write to a friend telling them all about the accident.

12 Ash Road
Seaford
Brookshire
SF3 7AW

10th July

Dear _____,

   You'll never believe it! We were playing football in the park when ...

PEARSON EDUCATION LIMITED
Edinburgh Gate, Harlow, Essex, CM20 2JE, England
and Associated companies throughout the World.

First published 2000
Third impression 2002
© Hilary Frost, Sarah Lindsay and Heather Painter 2000

Printed in China
GCC/03

ISBN 0 582 40799 0

Acknowledgements

We are grateful to the following for permission to reproduce poetry:

Cadbury Ltd for 'Penguin' by Rebbeca Clark from *Cadbury Book of Verse*; Mrs K
Froman for 'Friendly Warning' by the late Robert Froman; the author Trevor
Millum for 'Dick's Dog' © Trevor Millum

We have been unable to trace the copyright holders of 'Elephant' by Sonia Higgs and
'Thoughts in a Launderette' by Rita Ray, and would appreciate any information which
would enable us to do so.

The handwriting characters in this book were created using *Handwriting for Windows
2.0*. This product enables the user to create model handwriting in the size, colour and
style of their choice (including a dotted script). HfW2 runs on Windows 95 and above
and is available from KBER (Kath Balcombe Educational Resources). Please contact
Customer Services for details on 01743 356764.

Cover Bruce Coleman (Ingo Arndt)

The publisher's policy is to use paper manufactured from sustainable forests.